RED COLT

A Feathers in Hand Tale

Martha Frisbee

AuthorHouse™
1663 Liberty Drive
Bloomington, IN 47403
www.authorhouse.com
Phone: 1 (800) 839-8640

Published by AuthorHouse 11/30/2018

ISBN: 978-1-5462-4643-5 (sc)
ISBN: 978-1-5462-4644-2 (e)

Library of Congress Control Number: 2018907079

Print information available on the last page.

authorHOUSE®

Hundreds of years ago, wild horses ran in herds across the plains. Their many hooves sounded like thunder, and their manes and tails streamed in the wind like flames leaping from a fire. They feasted on the prairie grasses and snorted in the fragrances of the earth with their large fuzzy noses. Their hides were sleek in the summer and thick in the winter, and little birds gathered their shed out hair to build their nests.

In this time, a young girl named Feathers in Hand lived with her family and tribe near a river that wound through cottonwood trees. Saskatoon berries grew on large bushes nearby. Sunflowers, dandelions, and roses also bloomed, bringing all the creator's colors to the people. Feathers in Hand worked with her mother gathering berries and stalks from the tall grasses. Of course, the lovely feathers shed by molting birds were collected also. This was how Feathers in Hand received her name.

Summer was a busy time for the tribe. Actually, as Feathers in Hand grew older, it seemed that every season was busy. For now, there were berries to harvest, dry and store for Winter. There were tall grasses to gather for weaving baskets. A favorable hunt also provided meat to dry, skins and furs to tan, fat to render, and bones and organs. These were valued for making tools such as awls, hooks, water bottles, and other items.

Feathers in Hand learned many skills that were needed to live well on the plains. First, however, she had to collect as many berries as she could. They were abundant that Summer and having a good supply helped insure the tribe had plenty of food for the Winter.

The Summer of Many Berries and Good Hunting was a special memory for Feathers in Hand. This was also the Summer of Red Colt!

Months before, on a cold and crisp Spring morning, a mare called Runs Through Fire gave birth to a new baby boy! He had a short little mane that looked like a Mohawk hair-do, and his tail was short and curly. He was a lovely red colt with white legs and a white blaze. On the morning he was born, Feathers in Hand sat quietly nearby. She saw the colt work so hard to stand on his long legs. Runs through Fire nuzzled her baby and gave him his very first bath. Feathers in Hand slowly approached the horse and her colt. She touched both of them gently and spoke in soft kind words to Runs Through Fire. What a beautiful little Red Colt.

Life on the plains was full of meaning and lessons. There were happy moments and sad moments. All the times were important however; because, as the creator gave abundance to the people, they also received responsibilities. So, it was important to learn that the Earth gave balance--and needed it in return. Summers were not always bountiful. Hunts were not always successful. In times of scarcity, hard work from past seasons was appreciated. Stored fat, dried meats, berries, and nuts were highly prized, and the work that provided these things was much appreciated. Feathers in Hand learned that every task was important. Only when everyone contributed, did the people prosper.

Feathers in Hand also knew that a gift was a responsibility. A good hunt meant much work was needed to transform each buffalo into hides, meat, and tools. A big crop of berries meant much picking, spreading to dry, and storing in baskets. The finest gifts always brought the greatest responsibilities. Feathers in Hand learned this when, in the Summer of Many Berries, her father gave her Red Colt! (p. 9)

Receiving a horse was a very great honor. For Feathers in Hand, it meant that her father had given her the greatest gift a girl could receive. With a horse, she could command her future! She would be able to have her own lodge! She could travel great distances and hunt game. She could even ride with the men when they scouted buffalo! Of course, Red Colt came with a lot of responsibility. Her father knew she would need to feed and water her horse. Red Colt had to be groomed and trained. He needed a bridle and a blanket. All these things were now responsibilities of Feathers in Hand. Her father showed great trust, and she knew that caring for her horse would bring him joy and pride.

After much work, it was important to have a meal and share events of the day and stories from the past. Elders nodded knowing that children would grow still listening to the conversations and histories. Important life lessons were shared with the tribe. Stories of The Winter of Falling Stars, The Black Sun, The Summer of No Buffalo, and recently, The Horse that Ran Through Fire. The dark eyes of the storyteller twinkled in the firelight while he shared tales of victory and loss. Hope and bravery filled the hearts and imaginations of the young. As evening deepened, children slept. Eventually the embers of the fire died down, and all the people retired to their lodges.

As years passed, Feathers in Hand became an important woman in her tribe. The first birth she saw was Red Colt; now, she helped women of the tribe with their babies. She learned about many plants. Flowers, berries, and roots helped heal her people. She also had a strong spirit that helped protect the weak and wounded that she also cared for.

Feathers in Hand believed that her strong spirit was a gift from her father. As he died, he told her that his spirit would leave and hers would grow stronger. As she wept, he explained that death awaited all people, and tragedy came even to the greatest spirits just as fortune sometimes came to the unworthy. Balance and harmony were essential to all things. She had to accept rather than try to overcome.

Feathers in Hand was greatly blessed by her father. She found strength from his wisdom. She carried his memory and strength with her always, and she knew that a great joy would come to balance her sadness. She saw beauty in the lives of her people. She also saw beauty in the lives of her horses.

On a cold, crisp spring morning, a mare of Red Colt had a beautiful baby. She was a yellow filly with white legs just like Red Colt. The little horse struggled and finally stood up with her mother. Feathers in Hand admired the filly and knew she would be a beautiful Yellow Mare. She watched the horses as she sat quietly nearby.

Special thanks to Maverick, our Red Colt;

and Topaz, our Yellow Mare.

Thanks to the Bison, still living in Wyoming.

Thanks Charlie, for being the best travel buddy ever!

About the Author

Martha Frisbee is an avid traveler and culture collector. She has studied in Europe, Canada, and South America. Her fascination with Native cultures is heightened by each book, dance, painting, photo, and piece of handcrafted jewelry that she encounters. Among her trips, she has visited villages in Ecuador; lands of the Cheyenne, Kootenai, Flathead, and Blackfeet Indians; traveled up Montana's Bitterroot Valley, and enjoyed a special presentation and meal at Head-Smashed-in-Buffalo Jump (a Siksika World Heritage Site in Alberta, Canada). She is a graduate of North Carolina Wesleyan College where she studied Native American Literature with Dr. Chris LaLond, later majoring in Biology with a minor in Chemistry. She currently enjoys gardening, fishing, yarn crafts, and traveling with her husband, Charlie.

Printed in the United States
By Bookmasters